Mindful Moments

Mindful Moments

*Thoughts to Nourish
Your Body and Soul*

DEEPAK CHOPRA, MD

Illustrations by Cocorrina

Clarkson Potter/Publishers
New York

Breathe–

Reality is DIFFERENT in different states of consciousness. To REVISE your reality, look within.

In my stillness,
I am the eternal possibility.
In my movement,
I am the cosmos.

Infinite being is also
infinite love.

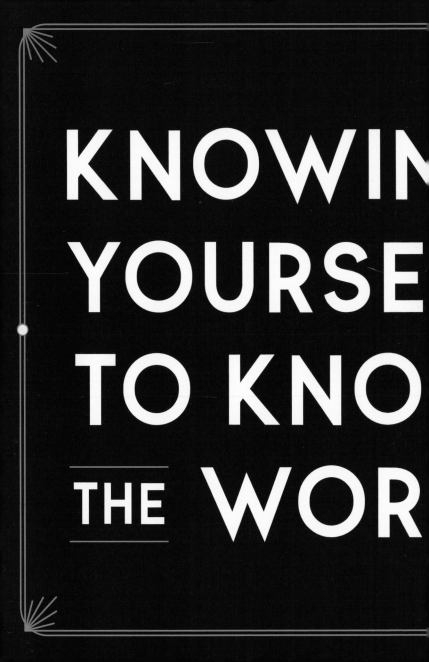

KNOWIN
YOURSE
TO KNO
THE WOR

IG
LF IS KEY
WING
LD.

The world outside your skin is as much you as the world inside. Your personal and universal bodies are equally yours.

There is no center of consciousness in the body because consciousness is not in the body. The body is in consciousness.

Gratitude is ABUNDANCE consciousness.

Intention with <u>LOVE</u> and detachment makes even the most <u>IMPROBABLE</u> happen.

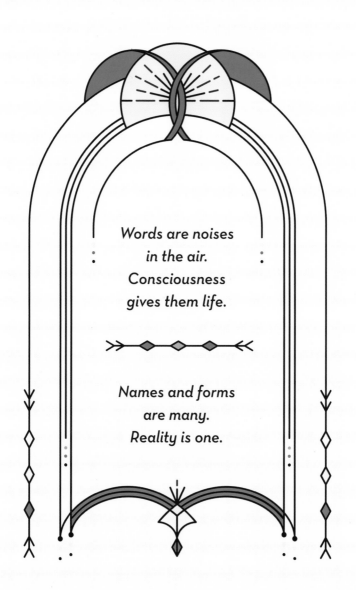

*Words are noises
in the air.
Consciousness
gives them life.*

*Names and forms
are many.
Reality is one.*

*Embrace the unpredictable
and the unexpected.
That is the path to your
infinite creativity.*

*If you want infinite energy,
focus on the infinite.*

BLISS, CONSCIOUSNESS, and LOVE are the essence of BEING.

Joy, ecstasy, and unbounded LOVE are the natural state of the unconditioned mind.

Awareness conceives, governs,
and sustains body and mind.
You need only not interfere with it.

Your personal desire is also
a manifestation of the total universe.

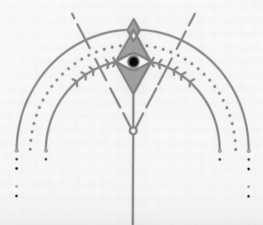

*Everything you call the "world," including
your own body, is sensations, images,
feelings, and thoughts in consciousness.*

———

*When you look at your body,
you are looking at your past.*

To love and to be loved—this is the most natural and spontaneous expression of our being.

Love is the
HIGHEST
intelligence.

*Everything perceived
as "outside" is sensations, feelings,
images, and thoughts within you,
and "you" has no location.*

*The observer has no location
in space or time. The terms inside
and outside do not apply.*

*Addiction is not getting enough
of what you don't want. It is being hooked
to a memory of pleasure that is now pain.*

---

*Fear is the memory of pain. Addiction is
the memory of pleasure. Freedom is beyond both.*

To SHIFT
your identity
to your
INNERMOST
being is
to affirm your
perfection.

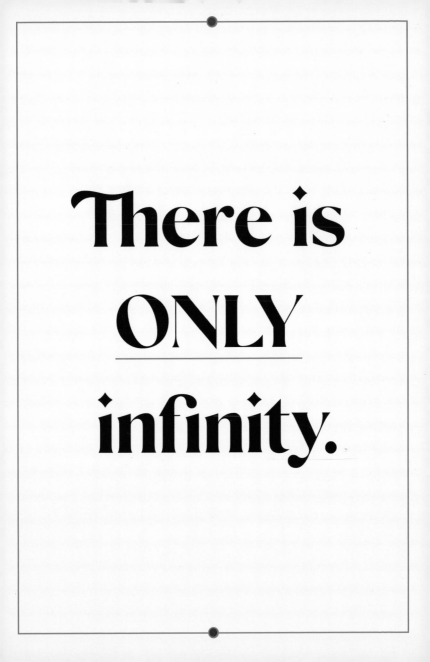

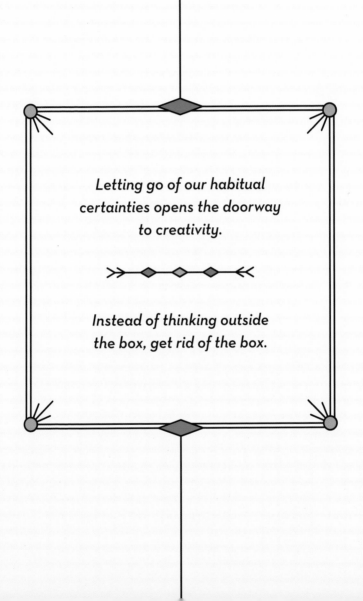

Letting go of our habitual certainties opens the doorway to creativity.

≫ ◆ ◇ ◆ ≪

Instead of thinking outside the box, get rid of the box.

Consciousness exists in every cell of our body and in every particle in the universe.

This moment is as it should be,
unless you think about it. This moment is
eternal before you label it.

———————

This is the moment of power.
Be the moment.

Every experience
creates its
own bodymind.
I experienced
childhood and
youth in different
bodies,
different minds.

Beyond LOGIC
is POETRY.
Beyond POETRY
is MUSIC.
Beyond MUSIC
is the DANCE.
Beyond the DANCE,
just LOVE.

*Pure consciousness is
the source of synchronicity
and meaningful coincidence.*

*As you rest in pure awareness
and watch synchronicity
unfold, "surrender to God"
takes on new meaning.*

The universe dances to a silent, abstract, mathematically perfect symphony in the cosmic mind.

———

The laws of physics are precisely fine-tuned for us to exist and even to allow us to discover those laws.

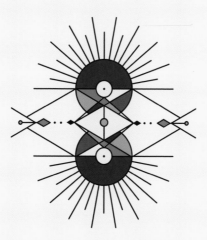

You CREATE your past and your future NOW.

Your senses send
electrical information
to your brain.
Your consciousness
converts that information
into a material universe.

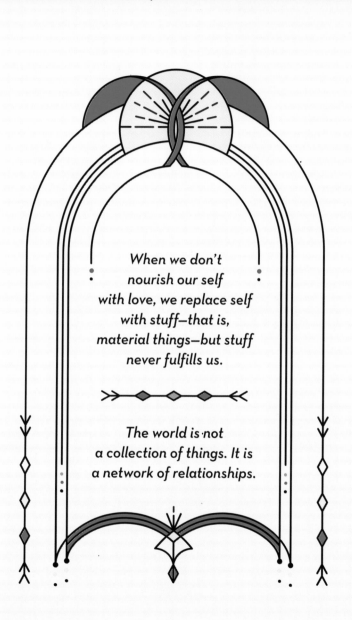

*When we don't
nourish our self
with love, we replace self
with stuff—that is,
material things—but stuff
never fulfills us.*

*The world is not
a collection of things. It is
a network of relationships.*

All form arises from the formless realm of potential forms, the source and origin of the universe.

Life as <u>LOVE</u>, compassion, <u>JOY</u>, equanimity, imagination, and <u>CREATIVITY</u> cannot be quantified by science.

Just as we have a body,
mind, and spirit, the universe
has a physical, mental,
and consciousness component.

People don't grow old; when they stop growing, they become old.

Our sense of self determines our experience of the world.

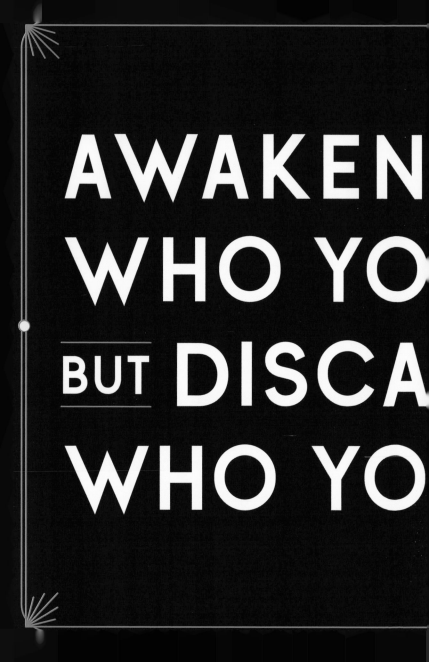

AWAKEN
WHO YO
<u>BUT</u> DISCA
WHO YO

ING IS NOT

U ARE,

RDING

U ARE NOT.

Love is the
EXPERIENCE
and knowledge
of one being
in many
appearances.

*Atoms die in waves
of potentiality. Waves are born
in atoms of actuality. The cosmos
reincarnates eternally.*

*Your physical form was
conceived in a wave of desire.
Desire is pure potentiality,
seeking manifestation.*

Just as a wave is a movement of the whole ocean, you are the energy of the cosmos.

Don't underestimate your power. Your inner potential and cosmic potential are the same field. The field is you and the universe, just as wave and ocean are one.

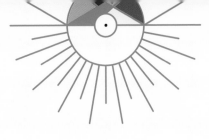

When you are
balanced in body,
mind, and spirit, you feel
joyful, energetic,
restful, alert, and
experience lightness
of being.

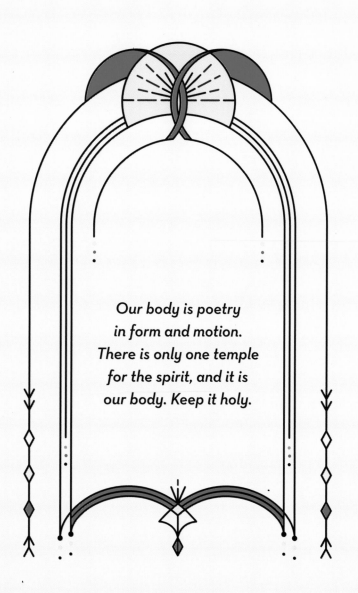

Our body is poetry
in form and motion.
There is only one temple
for the spirit, and it is
our body. Keep it holy.

We are the UNIVERSE dancing.

*Both mathematics and music are
the language of the universe, expressing
truth, harmony, and beauty.*

*Science is a spiritual quest
to know ourselves.*

What we do
to the world, we do
to ourselves.
Science based
on the objective
world as separate
from us is
dangerous.

Synchronicity, meaningful coincidence, good luck, creative response from the universe, and grace are synonymous terms.

*Humility, awe, wonderment,
and delight are qualities of spirit,
not just electrochemical events
in synaptic networks.*

*Nothing ever ceases to exist. Death is
incubation in the field of potentiality
until the next leap of creativity.*

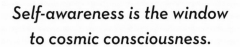

Self-awareness is the window to cosmic consciousness.

The simplest definition of spirituality is self-awareness.

Every moment is
a fork in the road.
The road you take
will shape your future.
Choose love over fear.

———

*Logic and rationality are
the language of the scientific mind.
Love and wisdom are the poetry
of the spiritual soul.*

≫ ◆ ◆ ◆ ≪

*If your reality is only rational,
and has no room for feelings
and the irrational, then
your humanity is incomplete.*

Love is
a quality
of AWARENESS
that allows
SOULS
to commune
with each
other.

Karma or choices in the past
create the situations of
the present. How we choose now is
a function of free will. To witness yourself
making choices is the beginning
of karmic freedom.

Between the banks of pleasure
and pain, the river of life flows.
The key is to let go and flow.

If you sacrifice your health to make money today, you will have to sacrifice your money to get health tomorrow.

*If you sacrifice the present
for the future,
you will never enjoy life,
for when the future arrives,
you won't be present.*

Being awake means that the best time of your life is neither behind you nor ahead of you, but now.

Consciousness is the organizing principle that transforms chaos into cosmos.

To BECOME
the consciousness
of that which
you witness
is LOVE.

God is the inconceivable truth in which we and the universe are happening.

I AM is all bodies
and all minds
in one consciousness,
one spirit.

The essence of our being
is eternal possibility.

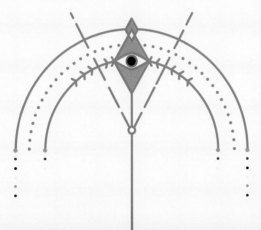

The law of least effort:
"Do less and achieve more."
Then graduate to "Do nothing
and achieve everything."

The law of least effort works
through choiceless awareness, plus
subtle intention, leading
to synchronicity.

A religious experience encompasses transcendence, love, compassion, humility, reverence for life, and loss of the fear of death.

Your ANCESTORS

are alive in every cell of your body as your genetic activity.

In every seed, there is the promise
of thousands of forests. So, too,
in desire is the seed of thousands
of manifestations.

As you witness yourself making
choices, you begin the process
of awakening.

*The ground of existence is not
inert emptiness, but a dynamic
field connecting all creation
in a single totality.*

*Random mutations in evolution
are reminiscent of quantum
uncertainty. Beyond chaos is
a creative organizing principle.*

Sensations and feelings in the body are the KEYS to intuition.

ILLNESS B
WITH "I."
BEGINS W

EGINS
WELLNESS
ITH "WE."

The fruit takes time to ripen and then falls suddenly. Enlightenment works in a similar way. There is always preparation and awakening.

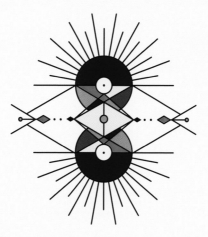

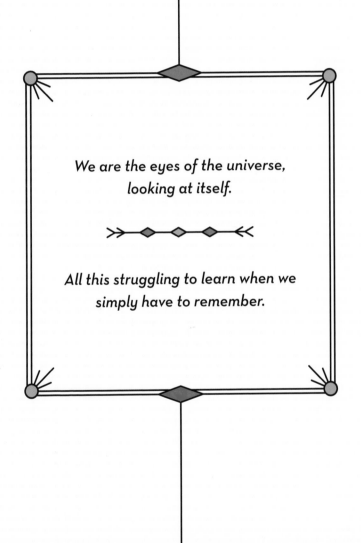

We are the eyes of the universe,
looking at itself.

All this struggling to learn when we
simply have to remember.

No matter what the situation,
there is a choice.

You will never trust your intuition
until you identify with it.
Self-esteem enters here.

**Every event has
innumerable
causes and leads
to innumerable effects.
Events and objects
are snapshots
of the universe in motion.**

The only
MADNESS
that is
sane is the
intoxication
of love.

Stop playing small.
You are divinity
in motion.

To own the world, see
infinite potential in all
situations at all times.

All boundaries are conceptual. The universe boundless outward in the cosmos, boundless inward in the atom.

Think cosmically, communicate globally, act locally, but with global and cosmic impact.

To be ALIVE is to be AWARE and PRESENT. Then every moment, every BREATH, is BENEDICTION, GRACE, and a MIRACLE.

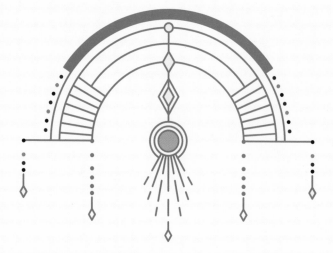

At the moment
of conception, you had
neither body nor
brain, but awareness
was present.

In the hall of mirrors,
I can see for miles.
Every demon, every enemy,
every torturer is me in disguise.

Through the mirror of relationship,
I see myself.

*We are the human activity
of the universe, and most of it is
unknowable. We cannot step outside
the universe to see it.*

*Everything in the visible world has its
roots in the formless invisible.*

Love can be
our RELIGION
beyond boundaries
if we live it,
BREATHE it,
experience it,
BECOME it.

Self-awareness
and compassion
ease our own suffering.

———

When your awareness is free, you know the entire universe as your body.

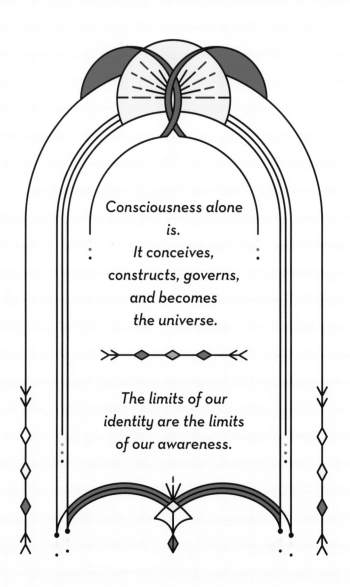

*Consciousness alone
is.
It conceives,
constructs, governs,
and becomes
the universe.*

*The limits of our
identity are the limits
of our awareness.*

The more universal or cosmic your sense of self, the bigger your world will be.

At all times, your world is a projection of yourself. Expansion of self to universal awareness is enlightenment.

AWARENESS is

a field in which

minds, bodies,

and universes arise

and SUBSIDE like

waves in an ocean.

Spirituality is not a contrived MOOD or behavior, but a simple, unaffected humanity.

*What we are looking for is
the one who is looking.*

*Only the witness of the mind
can know the mind.*

Peace can only be created
by those who are peaceful, and love
by those who have loved.

At all times, what we are aware of is
the qualities of our own consciousness.
The world is as we are.

The only sane
RESPONSE
to our
collective
insanity is
unconditional
LOVE.

*God is the infinite potential
in which galaxies and universes
arise from nothingness
and disappear into nothingness.*

*Only God exists. Everything
else is flux—the coming
and going of God.*

LOVE
is the
ultimate
TRUTH.

Lightness of being, <u>FLOW</u>, and joy are the outcome of letting go of what never was.

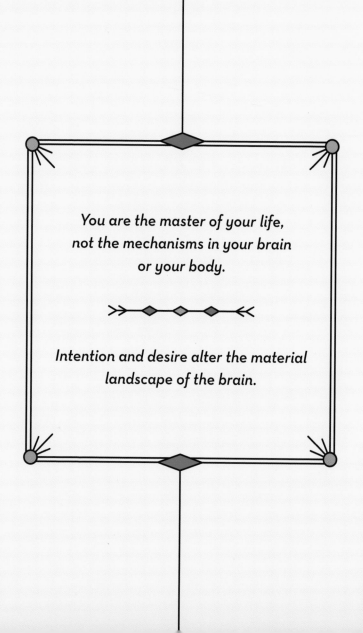

*You are the master of your life,
not the mechanisms in your brain
or your body.*

*Intention and desire alter the material
landscape of the brain.*

*Neurons and genes turn on and off,
depending on your choices.*

*Reclaiming consciousness is
nothing other than reclaiming
the power of choice.*

Angry people SHOUT, those in love **WHISPER,** those who are love become **SILENT.**

EACH
US IS
ONE N

*Religion has
an obligation not to contradict
the known laws of science.*

*Science has an obligation
not to reduce rich human
experience to raw data.*

Be a child, let go, allow the rhythms of nature to cradle you, and the universe will carry you wherever your dreams are cosmic consciousness.

If you obsess over whether you are making the right decision, you are basically assuming that the universe will reward you for one thing and punish you for another.

Atoms emerge from a void that is pure
potential. Thoughts emerge
from a void that is pure consciousness.

You are the growing tip of the cosmos,
the fresh spark of life being pushed
forward by all that exists.

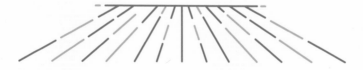

Your true self is the LIGHT of awareness that brings the world into manifestation.

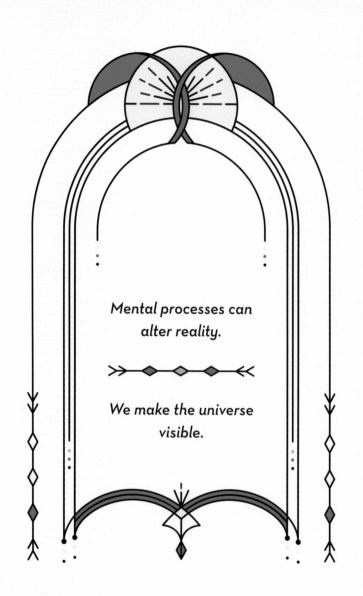

Mental processes can
alter reality.

>>> ◆ ◆ ◆ <<<

We make the universe
visible.

The universe has no fixed agenda. Once you make any decision, the universe works around that decision. There is no right or wrong, only a series of possibilities that shift with each thought, feeling, and action that you experience.

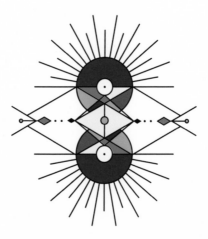

*Merely wanting bad things to stop
is not enough. You must intend
something new to replace the old.*

*Intention coming from
a deep level clears the way for its
own fulfillment.*

The world we experience
is a projection of images
in collective consciousness.

Consciousness is universal.
Perspective is personal.

The mind never sleeps. You can delegate CREATIVE solutions to it, even as your body sleeps.

AWARENESS

of self, of others, and of the world exists as sensations in the body. To know the world, feel your body.

Both religion and science are cultural mythologies with only partial glimpses of reality—one subjective, the other objective.

Science makes life comfortable. Spirituality makes life meaningful.

*Self-knowledge is the highest form
of knowledge.*

Be INNOCENT,
be SIMPLE,
be PRESENT,
and your
life will be
CHARMED.

Real happiness
or joy does
not depend on
circumstances.

———

*Consciousness cannot be
observed because
consciousness is the observer.*

Pain is not the same as suffering.
Left to itself, the body discharges
pain spontaneously, letting go
of it the moment that the
underlying cause is healed.
Suffering is pain that we hold on to.
It comes from the mind's mysterious
instinct to believe that pain is good,
or that it cannot be escaped,
or that the person deserves it.

A QUIET
mind is
more
powerful
than a
POSITIVE
mind.

An unseen, invisible reality
is the source of all visible
things, knowable through our
own awareness.

God is the unknowable
mystery of existence,
the mystery that is to be lived
and never solved.

The world is as we are.

*If you see your infinite
potential, the world is yours.*

Hope and despair are states of mind. <u>BEING</u> is beyond and free of both.

Good and evil
are expressions
of states of
mind. Evil can be
overcome
only from the
creative
womb of being.

Greatness is a choice.

*Every quality ascribed
to the physical universe, including
your own body, is a quality
in consciousness.*

CONSCIOUSNESS

is the

dimensionless

creator and

EXPERIENCER

of all dimensions.

SELF-POWER

is being
immune to
criticism
and flattery.

There is no flow of time.
There is only the flow of experience
around the still point of now.
Now never ends.

You walk in grace when you
surrender to now.

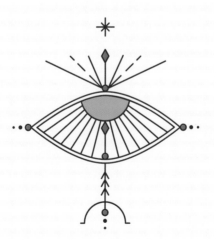

Money is the exchange of values in collective consciousness.

Wealth is a state of consciousness. Money is its bookkeeping symbol.

Sinner and saint are <u>STATES</u> of mind. Being is beyond both.

*The mind can know
the contents of the brain, but
the contents of the mind can't be
found in the brain.*

The only way to deal with change is to plunge into it, move with it, and join the dance.

Watch your thoughts, feelings, emotions, and reactions. Then watch the watcher of those thoughts, feelings, emotions, and reactions.

*Inner beauty is the light of love,
and when it radiates from you, you and those
around you will glow.*

*Peace can be created only by those
who are peaceful. A loving world will be
created by those who love.*

Everything we call "reality" comes to us through the <u>STRUCTURE</u> of our senses and our brain. It is a reflection of <u>OURSELVES</u>.

Everything that can happen has happened or is happening or will happen.

*The eternal invisible projects
as the temporal visible. Only the invisible is real.
Every time we reach for a creative idea,
we go to the same place where the universe
goes to create a rose or a galaxy.*

*Self-awareness is the highest knowledge
and transforms knowledge into wisdom.*

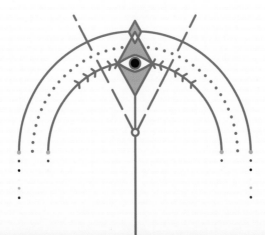

*In the absence of despair, there
is no need for hope. Being is
independent of both hope and despair.*

*Since your potential for
knowledge, creativity, and beauty is
infinite, settling for anything less
is a compromise.*

There is only ONE religion, and it is the religion of love.

Breathe.

Published in the United States by Clarkson Potter/Publishers, an imprint of Random House, a division of Penguin Random House LLC, New York.

clarksonpotter.com

CLARKSON POTTER is a trademark and POTTER with colophon is a registered trademark of Penguin Random House LLC.

ISBN 978-0-593-23402-0
eBook ISBN 978-0-593-23403-7

Printed in Malaysia

Illustrations by Cocorrina

Designed by Laura Palese and Nicole Block

Edited and compiled by Gary Jansen

10 9 8 7 6 5 4 3 2 1

First Edition